Becoming Your Own Key:

A guide to self-mastery, self-confidence, and

unlocking your unlimited potential.

Table of Contents

Introduction

Many people are dreamers, they have ideas, needs and wants that they wish to see as reality. They try their best to wake up each day, go out, work and come home. Some people are so interested in what they want that they work hard at their jobs believing they can get what they desire by working. They believe that if they are to be successful they must follow all the rules; some think that waking up every morning and going to work or going to college and obtaining a good job after graduation will bring them plenty of money to go off and fulfill their dreams.

These people are also often disappointed that though they do all of this, the reality is something completely different. They come to realize that no matter how hard they try, they have yet to fulfill their dream; even though they are working and even though they wake up and go off and follow the rules to a "T". Then after five, ten, fifteen years or more they either become disillusioned with the world or they decide to settle and to conform only to the life they did not want to begin with.

This is the life of many people in the world. It is a life of conformity and a waste of boundless potential. On the other hand, there is an elite group of people who seem to have the entire world under their thumb. Within this elite you find very passionate and happy people who are both content with themselves and the people around them. These people seem to be going forth and having their reality magically unfold before them. They make it seem as if there was no effort at all to achieve their goals. They are constantly creating new things and they are becoming richer and more powerful each day. But how is this possible? It's happening through the understanding of having dreams combined with the need and desire to improve one's life.

In response to this, most people would say: "As long as I am dreaming then I am also wanting to improve my life" and this is true, however it is only true in the conscious level of human mental and physical activity. When it comes to the subconscious level there is an entirely different mode and what is found is that most people do not have a desire or need to improve themselves subconsciously. It's not that they do not want this but over time through learned behaviors, and through self-deprecating actions and exposure to self-weakening ideals, people reprogram their subconscious mind. This reprogramming gets to a point where the subconscious is no longer providing a deep sense of personal improvement. Instead, a deep sense of insecurity and a deep-rooted inability to fully act and focus takes over. This is the truth that separates the elite from everyone else.

The elite have relearned how to reignite passions, fury, and courage in their subconscious mind thus giving them the ability to act. Have you ever been in a situation where there was something you consciously wanted to do, but deep within you there was something inhibiting you from taking action? Maybe there was a cute person you wanted to speak with and ask on a date, or maybe you wanted to ask for a raise, or you wanted to get more ketchup from a cash register at a fast food place. Regardless of what it was for you, if you answered yes and have been in similar situations then you have been a victim. You have been the victim of a weak subconscious and it is up to you to

make the decision to either stay the way you are or to take action

and move forward towards your destiny.

Chapter 1: Acknowledge Your Past

There are many experiences that cause a person to grow and experience life with a stronger ability to solve problems and bring strength to those around them. This is what acknowledging the past can do for you; doing this allows you to liberate yourself from what holds you back from seeing new opportunities. Part of acknowledging the past is learning how to let go. Before continuing, it is important to understand that the past is something that should not be taken for granted. The past is a tool for self-improvement. No one can hope to reach their full potential without first seeing where they come from. It is the past that allows a person to trace the steps of how they came to be.

By looking back into the past, you are able to see where your current beliefs and ideas about the world originate within your mind. And this is one of the keys to self-improvement and developing self-confidence. By seeing the origin of your beliefs, you can see both the advantages and disadvantages in your own world view and how helpful or useless such an idea may be in your life. After noticing the circumstances in which the information that powers your world view originated, you will be able to easily change from low level self-weakness to a high level of self-respect and mental liberation.

Overall it is important to recognize that only through first acknowledging and overcoming the hurdles of the past can one move forward and develop to the next level. It is also important for you to understand that you will never have full self-confidence until you develop the confidence to look and analyze your past. The only other option there is, if you choose to run away from your past is to continue to place yourself in the same situations that continue to plague your mind and life. Imagine a person who is always getting a new job. They start the job off fine and then within the first few weeks they are arguing with all their co-workers. Suddenly, their boss hates them. After that, they are either fired or they quit, then they find a new job, and the same thing happens again. To their distress they can't figure out why this keeps happening to them. They then try to explain it by thinking that perhaps it is the job or people who are causing the issue and that those people are absolute terrible humans. In my other books I usually mention that 99 percent of all human conflicts arise because of carelessness and misunderstanding.

Usually in a case such as this there is misunderstanding, but it arises from the fact that they can't understand the source of their perceived bad luck, which is just them not taking the time to sort out their past. Now this phenomenon is much more prevalent than most would think, and it applies in many different social settings, from friendships, jobs housing and roommate situations, vacation locations, acting and modeling careers and so forth. What happens is that a person moves to meet a new group of humans and within a set amount of time they are having issues or arguments with these people.

Then after that they leave that group, they find a new group, they get into conflict with those people and the process repeats over and over and these people are constantly doing this not knowing why it continues to take place. Such people usually have a high level of low confidence and do not have the ability to believe in themselves. Because of this, they are blinded by their self-deprecating nature and thus cannot see the root of the problem. However, that's what this book is for and that's the key to the first step in developing self-confidence and power, acknowledging the past.

The only way to acknowledge the past is to sit back and think about it, but you should not simply look at the past; you need to embrace it and take the time to look at the painful situations that you carry within. You must look at the situations that caused you to think of how things worked out for you and then have a conversation with yourself about the situations. Now this is a very scary situation because you must know yourself and to know yourself you need to connect with the present which means that you need to be open to new experiences and can question everything without all the unnecessary skepticism. This is because skepticism creates a natural barrier of information transference.

Now the cool thing about this is that anyone can do this. One of the easiest methods of connecting to yourself and acknowledging the past is to sit in quiet meditation. I have found that the Za-Zen meditation of the Zen Buddhists is a very effective method. There are of course many different approaches and styles of meditation and connection to the past. I have just found Za-Zen to be a very powerful force that allows you to see yourself for who you really are, and it forces you to acknowledge yourself and life experiences. By sitting in complete stillness and silence you become aware of the now. There is no past or future or even now, there is just existence. Then from there you will lose the connection of what you thought you were and truly start to see what you are. At first this can be frightening but it quickly changes to a feeling of freedom. Afterwards you continue to dig deeper into these elements of the past.

In the end, before doing anything else to build confidence it is very important to access and come to terms with your past because no matter how much progress in life you think you're making, if your past is not addressed you will become weak and the past will control your actions and how you view the world which can make you a very toxic individual without your knowing it.

Chapter 2: Acknowledge the Present

How does one acknowledge the present? The present is all that exists right now. As we speak, all that we are aware of is our present. There may be other things happening in other places completely unknown to us but that is not our present, that is the present of another being. Or more, that is the experience of the present through another being. Only when we are aware do we have the choice to experience the different possibilities of the present. The present moment for a tree or for a cat can be experienced together, but it can also be experienced separately. The tree can experience a separate present from you if you are not around. This is part of the meaning of the present.

To develop self-confidence, it is important to see that only the now exists. Everything that happened in the past is no longer here. There is of course cause and effect, because every cause has an effect and every effect creates a cause, but this is also a part of the present. That is why it is important to live in the now, because your actions and thoughts will always create the now. The now is all that exists and, in a way, the now is all there ever has been. The future is just a now that has yet to happen and to create a desirable future you must create a desirable now. That's all there is to this world. The world is just a moment. It is always a moment and a few moments are just parts of you.

The importance of acknowledging the present becomes beneficial once you begin to act in your life. You cannot fully take the appropriate amount of action to change your life if you are unaware of what is happening in your moment. Every person has their own moment because every person is experiencing their own life; and though you share moments with other people, it is still your moment. The same is true for the person you share the moment with; to them it is their moment. So, in the absolute there are two moments, in the relative to yourself there is only your moment, but in the ultimate absolute there is but one moment.

This is also how one can develop empathy and social intelligence. By accepting the present, you become aware that everyone else has their own moment which allows you to connect with people in their personal language while also still being true to yourself. When you don't live in the moment you are just in your head and all you can think about is yourself. This keeps you from experiencing the full scope of the events happening around you. Therefore, it causes you to have an ignorant mindset which over time creates a lack of confidence because you don't know what's going on, and you don't know what to do. To not live in the moment is to create a lock that keeps you from developing self-respect and self-confidence. Remember, the key to this is to acknowledge the present and you combine that with acknowledging the past.

Chapter 3: What You Think Is What You Are

"What you think is what you are"

This is a very important saying and this saying is actually a very important step in the development of self-confidence. In this saying there is a secret encoded message, which to those who have been working on self-confidence already, it may seem obvious, but to those who have not this is totally new information. Here is how it works:

1. What you think is what you are

2. What you are is what you become

3. What you become affects how you act

If you think in a manner that is self-deprecating then you become someone with self-hate, and when you become such a person you become blind to the opportunities in front of you. You become blind to love, compassion, fun, adventure, and you lack the ability to do whatever the hell you want. This is what happens when you think in such a manner which is why it is important to be aware of your thoughts. If you are not then it leads to weak relationships, a weak job life, a weak social life, weak ambition, and a significant increase in ignorance of yourself and the world around you.

An example of a person who lacks this self-awareness is someone who thinks that everyone or everything is out to get them. No matter what, they are always in a state of fear, even if there is nothing to be fearful of. This fear stems from a deep-rooted lack of confidence which may have developed as early as childhood because of how their parents raised them, or because of some traumatic event in their life. These later leads such a person to believe that they can only depend on themselves for nurture and security, which is of course incorrect because humans are social creatures, however this is what they have learned.

Another example is when someone says that they do not like to ask for help, or that they do not need other people. What they are really saying is that they are insecure and that if they asked for help they are afraid their insecurity will be revealed to the people involved. Now this is something that happens without their knowing because it is a subconscious insecurity. Consciously, they may just see themselves as simply a little prideful or stubborn, but, it is insecurity at the deepest roots. This happens because over time there was something that triggered and programmed this sense of insecurity within the minds of these people. This affects how one thinks, and as I said before, what you think is what you are. What you think subconsciously is what you are, and what you think consciously is also what you are.

If your conscious mind thinks different than your subconscious mind then you are not aligned and have inner conflict, which creates insecurity throughout your being and causes your actions to be that of low confidence. The way that most people deal with this is through consciously presenting themselves as strong individualistic people on the outside, who needs to control and analyze every element of their life. This usually causes hyper-analyzation which stresses and tires the mind, which further causes the mind to shut down, or explode. When this shutting down materializes in the physical form it comes in the form of running away from problems, unhealthy forms of social isolation, and an inability to make effective decisions in everyday life. The way to stop all of this is through understanding the statement above, "what you think is what you are." Once you understand this statement you will understand that the subconscious mind is the root of our deepest thoughts and beliefs, and if you reprogram the subconscious mind you can reprogram your entire life. Remember consciously thinking a certain way does not work. It may work for a little while, but it is not enough.

An example of a person who has mastered this step is genuinely happy with their life and displays a sense of appreciation and gratitude. It is important to understand that you can still have boastful displays of your possessions and be such a person; but what makes someone like this person who has mental solitude is the fact that their boasting is not out of insecurity. Instead, it is out of pure joy and happiness for what they are doing. An example of this would be a very famous rapper who has millions of dollars and everyday he posts on Instagram or Facebook. This rapper who earned his/her way into riches and fame, is having fun and simply is living his/her life. Those who are envious of him/her usually dismiss his/her boasting as weak insecurity but, the rapper is just showing off because it's fun and it's another way enjoying his/her life.

Another example could be a person who enjoys meeting people, going on adventures, and having fun. To many people this person seems oblivious to the world around her/him but, she/he is one of the few elites to truly see the world as it is. Because of that receptivity to happiness she/he can get what she/he desires. This desire comes from a deep inner desire which emanates from a subconscious that is happily and naturally aligned with the conscious mind leading to a healthier body, sharper mind, and more open connection with people.

In all essence, think in a positive manner but not only that, become aware of the signs of insecurity self-deprecating tendencies and low self-esteem.

These are some of the signs each of which have many sub-signs:

- Headaches

- Constant unexplainable irritability

- Constant conflicts with others

- Sense of loneliness

To combat this and develop a thinking that makes you a better person you must accept who you are as you are now. Then take the time to look at your strengths and weaknesses then go further and use active meditation. You can write letters to yourself and start a gratitude journal where you write down at least five things a day that you have gratitude for and then overtime these new concepts of strength, abundance, and gratitude will seep into your subconscious. This can take anywhere from a day to many months. If you keep up with it, then you are guaranteed to change and develop traits of active, noticeable, confidence that you as well as the people in your life will come to see.

This may be hard at first, but it is a skill that must be developed and practiced if you wish to have self-confidence and respect. Once you have this you can think for yourself and not care what other people think about you because you will be able to freely live your life with your thoughts that build you to a level of personal security.

Chapter 4: How You Act Is What You Attract

"Thoughts Are Action"

This part of the book is only able to be truly understood once you're able to work on this. I genuinely do not believe that you are able to change how you act until you acknowledge your past, acknowledge the present, and apply the idea of "what you think is what you are." The way you are able act directly affects what comes to you. This action is something that changes moment to moment as humans have an average of tens of thousands of thoughts in a day. Many of these thoughts and actions are of the subconscious nature so many of your actions are also subconscious, and many of your conversations are as well. When you have a strong, happy, and confident subconscious conversation or experience with another person then everything you do will work out fine.

To change actions from a negative low confidence action to a positive high confidence action takes a little work, but once you start it becomes more natural until eventually the high confidence person with a beautiful mind is all you are. If that is all you are then that means you are everything, because you can confidently interact with all things. To effectively interact with everything is to effectively connect with everything. Below are different techniques used to change your actions which aid in transmuting your energy of low confidence into an energy of high confidence.

Social Self Preparation:

This is a form of preparation in how to communicate with other people to better prepare yourself for interaction. This is something you do when you are first starting out with communicating and building self-confidence. After a while it becomes natural to the point that you don't recognize you're doing it; and eventually it gets to the point that you've adapted to it so well that it makes you open to learn new forms of communication. So, what you do is take the time to look at past situations of interaction and create hypothetical situations in your mind where you imagine being in a certain position. It is actually a very fun mental activity because you ask yourself what you would do or what you would say in certain situations. And if you really don't know what you would do then you would just say something no matter how ridiculous it sounds then imagine what the cause and the effects of such a statement would be. With this you can imagine yourself in any type of way you want because it is in your mental realm. You do not have to worry about your thoughts and actions affecting other people; since you're specifically in an experimental mental realm created for the practice of social interaction.

The Game of Rejection Confidence:

Another way to build confidence is by viewing confidence as a game. This method takes a lot more energy and effort than the other method above, but it is a lot more rewarding and fun. It builds your confidence around other people. It is a great remedy for people who are not confident in expressing themselves to other people or whose confidence is so low that they cannot ask for what they want. It is also effective for people who can't speak their mind, or for people who are indecisive.

This "game" is really a remedy for many things in life but most importantly interactions with people. Interacting with other people is both a strong tool to gauge confidence as well as one of the most effective ways to create confidence. It is just as important to look within yourself as it is to look outside of yourself, because people are mirrors and the way they interact with you is the way your subconscious mind has allowed them to. This is because the majority if human conversation and interaction does not come from the mouth but from the subtle and subconscious elements.

To play the game you must do this. Think of questions or actions that you would not normally request or consider, and you write them down on notecards or slits of paper. I would create at least fifty of these at first, though you can go further if need be. If fifty is too much for you to do right now, then just start with five. After doing all of that you would then put them in a hat, jar, or bowl, then mix them up and draw once a day. Whatever you pull out you would have the task of attempting that request for the entire day. The object of the game is for you to get someone to tell you "no." It is to remove your fear of rejection and to make you understand that rejection and being told no is not bad and will not hurt you. If by the end of the day you did not get someone to tell you "no" then you lose for that day. You only win once you are rejected.

If someone tells you "yes" to the first thing you drew, then you will need to draw again, and you will keep drawing until you get someone to tell you "no." This is surprisingly difficult to do because people will say yes more than they will say no. People are very willing to help people or even entertain certain actions or ideas in their life. This is because humans are naturally open and curious creatures, so it is much more difficult to get a "no" than a "yes." Eventually, you will get a "no" and once that happens you'll experience everything that comes with it. In time, you will rid yourself of the fear of rejection, which is what holds you back from having self-confidence. This is a way to see rejection. It is simply something that does not matter and when you dwell on it too much you waste a lot of mental energy.

I myself have used this "game" since I was a child. This is what some Children already do when they are testing their parents. They are testing to see what they can get away with, and they even ask the same questions over and over as well. As you get older, the only difference is that you have more things you can ask because you have more knowledge and a better grasp of the established rules of society. Over time playing this game makes it easier to change the way you act because now you are acting on what you want and not on "what if they say no?" Or "what if someone judges me because of this?" Or "what will happen if?" Now you are no longer confined by such self-limiting thoughts. This in turn connects you to your true confident self. So, go forth and use this game. It's fun and very fulfilling.

Go and create something:

Another method of building confidence is to create something. It does not really matter what it is that you create, or how great it is, it just matters that you are using your mental and physical strengths combined. You could create poetry, you could make a checkers board out of wood, you could be very into creating codes for computers. Or maybe you like to paint or draw or play guitar and come up with your own songs. Maybe you like to cook and just experiment for fun. It does not matter what you create, just create something. Ask yourself what you want to do and if you don't know what you want to do then just talk to yourself about it or just create something at random.

Acting in a random manner is very important for creating mental strength and self-confidence. Our society likes to teach us that being random and unpredictable is a bad thing, but it is not. It's fun to do and it is what gives you a unique perspective on the world. Randomness can also unlock new levels of personal fun and joy rather than always having other people involved. When other people become involved your random nature will draw people into your world. This is because everyone enjoys visiting other worlds. It is refreshing and fun. Not only that, but you can connect with people easier thus allowing you into their world too.

Chapter 5: Accept Your Goals and Go Forth

In this chapter you will learn how to accept your goals and go forth to create your life of confidence. It is not recommended that you read this chapter until you have read and understood the contents of the previous chapters. Those chapters are the keys to creating the mental fortitude needed for living a life full of high self-esteem and personal confidence. After that, this chapter shows you tips on ways to apply everything in your everyday life as well as effective ways to accept your goals with 100 percent confidence and faith that they will happen.

Accepting goals is perhaps the most difficult thing to do to build and maintain confidence, because the act of accepting a goal means that you want it to happen and you are acting on it. If you are not acting on your goals, then you have not truly accepted it, or else it would occupy a part of your personality and life. It would not just be in the mental realm, but it would be in action and once it's in the material world you would continue to reach it. To accept your goal is to finally have control over your life. No one can take your goals from you and no one has the power to stop you from reaching your goals unless you allow them to do so.

Your goals originate from your mind and you are the one who wants to do it. That is how you must look at it. You are the one who wants to do it, YOU ARE THE ONE WHO WANTS TO DO IT. No one else can do it for you. You can have someone help you but, in the end, it's up to you to reach that goal. Now it is important to realize that there is no issue in having assistance on your path to fulfilment; after all, humans are social creatures. Deep down we all want someone to help us at some point. This comes from our early dependence on parents, specifically from the infant stage to around five years old. This point is important to remember when building your new life.

So how do you create goals and how do you decide what they will be?

The first thing you will want to do is figure out what it is that you want to do. Some of you will say "I don't know, I have no drive so I'm not sure." If that is you, stop right now and tell your ego to shut up. That is your ego and we don't have time for such negative thinking, you're trying to live a life of fun and happiness, not one of ego filled toxicity and negativity. So, what you need to do is first look deep within yourself and analyze the things that you have enjoyed doing in the past. Think about absolutely anything that you had fun with in the past or experienced positive emotions from. Then analyze that and think what it is about that specific subject that made you happy in the first place.

After you have done this try to see what you want to recreate or how you would like to create the feelings that existed before. Goals are things which you would like to work towards that improves and enriches your life. It is not only limited to enriching your life, but they can enrich the lives of other people as well. Someone simply hearing about your goals could become inspired to create their mark on the world too.

After looking at the feeling that you would like to recreate think about the intended result. What is it that you intend to cause. What are the intended effects of your goal? Look at all possible outcomes even the ones where you think something could go wrong. And after looking at all the outcomes that you could think of, discard any of the negative and fear inducing outcomes and focus only on the positive outcomes. After that, choose the top three outcomes that you would like to see happen, and then choose the top outcome that your 100 percent want to happen. After that only think of that outcome and the positive effects it would have for you and other people as well.

Next revisit the negative outcomes and think of what you would do if you were in that situation. This is a form negative positivity, and it causes you to see a possible negative outcome; at least what you perceive as possible. If you say it's not possible then it's not possible. It allows you to see this "possible" outcome and think of what you would do if such an outcome were to happen. That way you are prepared and can easily adapt to any challenges on the way to your goal. Once that happens you can be assured that your goal is going to be reached even if there is a setback (the negative possibility).

After all this think of the desired outcome once again and know that it is going to happen. You can have a plan if you want but the key is to just know it's going to happen. Don't worry too much on the logistics; all you need to do is be sure of yourself and then take the appropriate action for it to happen. When I say take the appropriate action for it to happen; I mean take the action needed for it to be true. Don't act contradictory to your goal because then it's not going to happen. So many people take actions that completely contradict their goal and then they wonder why their goals never come to fruition. NEVER DO ANYTHING THAT WILL GO AGAINST YOUR GOAL!

An example of a contradictory action would be if you wanted a new car, you know that within a certain amount of time the car would come to you. You would have the money and you would be able to buy the car without any issue. Now the actions that get you the money are what matters. Let's say you decide to go and shoot someone for no reason, that action is in direct contradiction to you being able to get the car because you're not going to get it. Either you're going be dead because someone hunted you down for revenge or you're going be in jail which means you're not going get the car!!

Remember always act with intention and your goals will start to come into physical form.

Once you clearly know your goals you will have confidence, but what happens after you obtain self-confidence is up to you. You will need to have the ability to own and keep your confidence and that is why you must first acknowledge your past and present. Realize that what you think is what you are and how you act is what you attract because then you will have your own power.

To conclude, it is important to remember that self-confidence and power is something that can instantly be developed. The key is to accept that you need to improve, and the opportunity will instantly arrive!!

I wish you GOOD LUCK!!!

Made in the USA
Middletown, DE
13 August 2021

45958372R20024